MW00583795

SEISMIC PHILANTHROPY

HOW TO ACHIEVE EARTH-SHATTERING HIGH-IMPACT RESULTS WITH YOUR GIVING

BEN KLASKY

Published by Peabridge Press
PO Box 42133, Arlington, VA 22204

Book and cover design by Rhombus, Inc.

ISBN 978-1-950184-01-9 (pbk.)
ISBN 978-1-950184-00-2 (ebk.)

Printed in the United States of America

10 9 8 7 6 5 4 3 2 1

PEABRIDGE
PRESS

To Mom and Dad for teaching generosity

To Lisa for the epic journey

To Jake and Eli for shaking up our world

CONTENTS

SEISMIC PHILANTHROPY

THE ROAD TO SEISMIC

The proliferation of automobiles in the early 20th century made people's lives more convenient but also created serious new safety hazards. A simple innovation that has saved millions of lives is the concept of painting lines on the pavement to help cars stay in their lanes. There is disagreement as to who first painted centerlines on highways, but most roads lead to Edward Hines. Hines was appointed to serve as a road commissioner in Detroit's Wayne County, alongside Henry Ford. According to legend, Hines was struck with the idea to paint lines down the center of the road in 1911, after watching a horse-drawn milk wagon leak a line of milk down the street.[1]

By the mid 20th century, road centerlines had become commonplace, but Dr. John Van Nostrand Dorr was not satisfied. Dorr had led a successful career as an engineer and inventor, and had established a family foundation. He was an inventive man, who had worked as a teenager with Thomas Edison in his New Jersey laboratory.[2] Dorr had observed that drivers hugged centerlines during poor driving conditions, which led to unnecessary head-on collisions. He theorized that painting a white line along the outside shoulders of highways would save lives.[3]

His first action was to write to his state's highway commissioner suggesting the idea of a shoulder line, but he received no response. The following year, Dorr wrote a letter to his local newspaper outlining the concept and offering to fund a test site. Soon afterwards, Connecticut conducted a field test on a portion of the Merritt Parkway and the results were promising. This prompted both Connecticut and New York to perform a more extensive test which resulted in a 55% reduction in accidents and injuries.[4]

Despite these statistics, highway officials throughout the country refused to take action. Some balked at the expense of painting shoulder stripes, which cost up to $150 per mile at the time (over $14,000 per mile in today's dollars).[5]   Others were skeptical of the concept. Some California officials feared that motorists would drive to the right of the shoulder line, mistaking it for a centerline, and placing drivers and passengers at even greater risk.[4]

Shoulder lines continued to be controversial for years, and the Dorr Foundation never wavered from its commitment to the issue. It organized extensive field studies that were overseen by the Highway Research Board and National Academy of Sciences. The foundation also served as a clearinghouse for information about shoulder lines, and issued bulletins sharing the results of new tests. And it spent considerable effort lobbying local, state and federal government officials—as high up as the White House. After a decade of continued effort, the foundation had proven the importance of shoulder lines, which gained universal public acceptance and application.[4]

The Dorr Foundation did not have a particularly large endowment, yet it was able to have a remarkable impact saving countless lives over the years. The foundation's success can be attributed to the following:

1) It was laser focused on an issue.

2) It developed a plan, which involved multiple strategies including funding, research, and advocacy.

3) It remained committed to this cause over time. The foundation was "all in" and invested its wealth, energy and political connections toward the problem.

4) It course-corrected its strategies based on input it gathered from partners in the

field such as researchers and government agencies.

This book is for people who, like Dr. Dorr, want to be intentional and strategic with their giving. It's for people who hope to have a remarkable impact in the world and strive for their philanthropy to be seismic.

Seismic is earth shattering. Ground breaking. World-changing.

Seismic makes waves. Shakes things up. Creates a tectonic shift. Breaks down walls.

Don't expect the journey as a **Seismic Philanthropist** to be easy. There will be many challenges along the way (as outlined in Part II), but these can be overcome by using the Epicenter Giving System™ (detailed in Part III). This system helps people experience more joyful and rewarding lives, by creating the positive change they envision in the world.

I. WHY GIVE

———————————

At first blush, giving away large sums of money to others beyond one's family may seem peculiar, but it is actually one of the most natural acts a person can do. Research has shown that being charitable not only helps those who receive gifts, but also benefits those who give.

We are in the midst of the largest inter-generational transfer of wealth ever. Over the next thirty years, $30 trillion is expected to pass from baby boomers in the US alone—that's an average of $240,000 per household. This trend, as well as a robust economy over the last few decades, has left many individuals with more resources than they need in their lives.

In his 1889 "Gospel of Wealth" Andrew Carnegie wrote that there are only three ways to handle surplus money: 1) spend it; 2) leave it to family; or 3) donate it for public purposes. He asserted that thoughtful individuals will not pass "the curse of the almighty dollar" to their children, because it spoils them and makes them less likely to serve others. He also warned against waiting until death to donate money because large estates are heavily taxed, there is less control over the results, and it puts off the good that can be done.[6]

Carnegie's beliefs resonate with many people of means, who find themselves wanting to share some of their resources to help others. This is not a new phenomenon. People in their shoes (or leather sandals if one looks back into history) have had similar feelings for thousands of years.

GIVE FOR OTHERS

Some feel a moral obligation to give, which can stem from their spiritual upbringing. A number of religions encourage generosity which is known by many names, including tithing or making an offering (Christianity); tzedakah (Judaism); zakat (Muslim) and dana (Hinduism). Regardless of what it is called, the act of giving to others is a timeless concept:

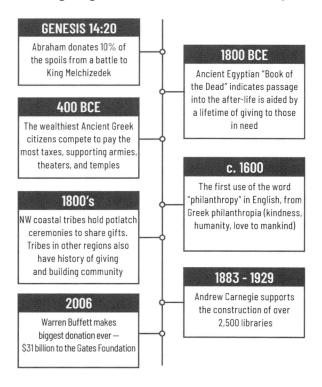

GENESIS 14:20
Abraham donates 10% of the spoils from a battle to King Melchizedek

1800 BCE
Ancient Egyptian "Book of the Dead" indicates passage into the after-life is aided by a lifetime of giving to those in need

400 BCE
The wealthiest Ancient Greek citizens compete to pay the most taxes, supporting armies, theaters, and temples

c. 1600
The first use of the word "philanthropy" in English, from Greek philanthropia (kindness, humanity, love to mankind)

1800's
NW coastal tribes hold potlatch ceremonies to share gifts. Tribes in other regions also have history of giving and building community

1883 - 1929
Andrew Carnegie supports the construction of over 2,500 libraries

2006
Warren Buffett makes biggest donation ever — $31 billion to the Gates Foundation

History aside, perhaps the most important reason to get serious with philanthropy is to address chronic problems facing the world today, such as these:

- Over half of all deaths in low-income countries stem from nutritional deficiencies, communicable diseases and conditions arising during pregnancy and childbirth. By contrast, less than 7% of deaths in high-income countries are due to such causes.[7]

- Climate change is impacting our ecosystems and communities. 60% of the planet's vertebrate populations have died off in the last 40 years.[8] Over 21 million people are displaced annually because of weather hazards related to climate change.[9] And it is projected that 70% of the world's coastlines will be impacted by rising sea levels (up nearly 4 feet by the end of this century)—leading to flooding, erosion, and destruction of infrastructure.[10]

- On any given night in the United States, more than half a million people experience homelessness. Over a third of these individuals are living on the streets or in other places not meant for habitation. Families make up a full third of the homeless population, meaning there are many homeless children as well as adults.[11]

- A student drops out of high school every 26 seconds in the U.S. High school dropouts commit about 75% of our nation's crimes, and earn hundreds of thousands of dollars less than high school graduates over the course of their lives. An astounding 33% of minority students (compared to 8% of white students) attend "dropout factories"—schools where under 60% of students graduate.[12]

By tackling issues such as these or countless others that are solvable within a lifetime, philanthropy has an incredible opportunity to make a difference.

GIVE FOR YOURSELF

Beyond helping others and the planet, charity also benefits the donor. Consider a scenario in which two business partners sell their company and each earns $100 million from the deal. One of them (Kyle) wants to keep his money, and the other one (Charlotte) plans to be charitable with her windfall. In this example, Kyle keeps 100% of his profits for himself. Charlotte chooses to give away half her earnings to charity (maybe she sets up a donor-advised fund or a family foundation). The highest federal income tax rate is currently 37% and state income taxes vary tremendously from 0% to over 13%. To keep things simple, since actual tax laws are a bit more complex, let's assume that Kyle and Charlotte's total tax burden is 40%.

In keeping all his earnings, Kyle can expect to pay $40 million in taxes, and be left with $60 million in cash. Since donations are not taxed, Charlotte can expect to pay $20 million in taxes, and be left with $30 million in cash.

Charlotte will have half the remaining disposable income of Kyle. There are also two other key differences that they can expect:

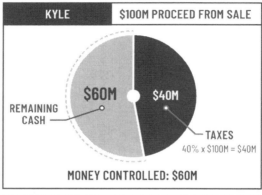

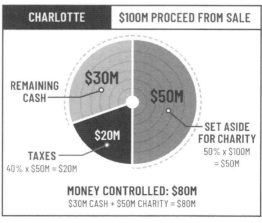

- Kyle will pay an extra $20 million in taxes.

- Charlotte will retain control of $20 million more than Kyle, because she will manage the money she sets aside for charity in addition to her remaining cash.

There's also a good chance that Charlotte will be happier than Kyle. The phrase "money can't buy happiness" may be true—unless the money is spent on someone else. In academic studies, participants who were randomly assigned to spend money on others experienced greater happiness than those assigned to spend money on themselves.[13] Neuroscience also reveals that we experience pleasure when acting generously. According to one study, giving to others stimulates the same "reward pathway circuits in our brain that are triggered when we eat, receive money, or have sex."[14]

There are other personal benefits to being charitable. Giving together can deepen family bonds, connect different generations, teach perspective and life skills to younger family members, and create friendships outside the family.

II. BARRIERS TO GIVING

I f charity is so rewarding, then why aren't people giving more aggressively? One major barrier is how difficult it is to give away money effectively.

Pretend that you are given $100 million and two assignments to complete in the next 24 hours. First, invest half of the money wisely for your future. Then donate the second half to high quality charitable work. The first task would be easy, because there is a robust and highly evolved marketplace of wealth managers standing by to help with such investments. It's possible to allocate $50 million across a diversified portfolio of mutual funds in just minutes. But the second task is a much greater challenge for a variety of reasons.

OPTION PARALYSIS

There are over 1.5 million registered charities in the US, and the largest ratings organization has only evaluated about 9,000 of them, or six-tenths of one percent. Deciding which charities to support can be overwhelming. For example, consider trying to find a nonprofit that is working on a cure for cancer. A Google search for "cancer charity" produces hundreds of millions of results. A search for "cancer" in one of the leading nonprofit databases produces over 8,500 cancer-related charities. Even a search as specific as "New York breast cancer research" produces over 500 results in that same database.

Having too many choices leads to poorer outcomes, despite the widely-held opposite belief. Researchers from Columbia and Stanford found that people were more likely to purchase gourmet jams or chocolates or to undertake optional class essay assignments when given a limited set of six choices rather than a more extensive array of 24 or 30 choices. Moreover, participants actually reported greater satisfaction with their selections.[15]

WEALTH ADVISORS CAN HELP, BUT...

Given the challenges in selecting nonprofits, many people turn to a trusted financial advisor for help. Wealth managers have been criticized in the past for having reverse incentives when it comes to their clients' charitable giving. Since they are hired to grow investments, how can advisors possibly be motivated to give money away? However a recent study indicates that wealth advisors are making notable progress in helping clients with philanthropy.[16]

Resarchers found that nearly all wealth advisors (91%) now believe it is important to have philanthropic conversations with their clients. And in these conversations, the vast majority of advisors encourage their clients to donate money to charity. Advisors and clients also report that these conversations are helping them build deeper relationships with each other.

Despite this good news, the study also suggests room for improvement: Less than half of clients are fully satisfied with these philanthropic conversations—in part because advisors tend to emphasize technical topics (e.g. taxes and wealth structuring) instead of focusing on their clients' philanthropic goals and passions. As can be seen in the following table, wealth advisors often misunderstand why some high-net-worth clients avoid charity.

WHY CLIENTS SHY AWAY FROM CHARITY	
WEALTH ADVISORS BELIEVE THEIR HIGH-NET-WORTH CLIENTS FEAR:	**HIGH-NET-WORTH CLIENTS** ACTUALLY FEAR:
⊙ They may not be left with enough money for themselves	⊙ Their gifts may not be used wisely by nonprofit recipients
⊙ They may not have enough money to leave to their heirs	⊙ They lack knowledge about or connection to a charity
⊙ They are not wealthy enough to give charitably	⊙ They will receive increased donation requests from others

UNCLEAR MARKET SIGNALS

I n financial markets, there are clear signals as to how investments are performing: stock prices rise and fall; profits or losses are reported quarterly. But with nonprofit work, it can be harder to determine if one's investments are paying off. Although there are promising recent innovations, most ratings organizations have historically tried to measure the success of nonprofits by looking at how much money is spent on overhead.

This concern about overhead is not shared by the corporate world. It's hard to imagine an investor in a for-profit company insisting that her money not be spent on rent, sales, or management salaries. Business author Jim Collins uses college sports to illustrate the failed logic in focusing on nonprofit overhead.[17] When teaching at Stanford, Collins noted that the university pays its athletic coaches higher salaries than typical Division I schools. However, Stanford also holds the all-time record for winning NCAA titles. In the most recent year, its athletes also had an overall graduation rate of 97%, with 17 of its teams boasting a 100% graduation rate.[18] For those who care about an athletic program's results (measured by division titles and graduation rates) then coaching salaries are not a useful measure of success.

Dan Pallotta (of Breast Cancer 3-Day walk and AIDS Ride fame) has made perhaps the most passionate appeal to shift our thinking away from overhead. 4.5 million viewers have watched his TED Talk entitled "The Way We Think About Charity Is Dead Wrong." Pallotta shares his personal story of being forced to shut down his company, when sponsors abandoned his events because he was branded with a "too much overhead" label. This happened despite the fact that his events produced the most funding in support of breast cancer and AIDS research at the time. Pallotta implores donors to stop worrying about frugality, and start helping charities invest in high-impact leadership, marketing and delivery systems to achieve big goals and accomplishments.

FAILING TO LISTEN TO CONSTITUENTS

Steve Jobs once famously said "A lot of times, people don't know what they want until you show it to them."[19] This may be true for innovative technologies, but obtaining the best results in the social sector typically requires that funders listen to, empower, and collaborate with those on the ground. Stories abound of well-funded projects that missed the mark by failing to gather input from those being served: medical professionals wearing alien-looking hazmat suits that scared Ebola-infected individuals, causing them to flee the area and further spread the disease; healthier breeds of plants that were rejected by malnourished families because the new crops looked or smelled different; malaria bednets that were used instead as fishing nets or avoided altogether because the color of the nets looked like death shrouds in some cultures.

THE MOST POPULAR PERSON AT THE BALL

Another barrier to giving is the distorted power structure between funders and nonprofits, which can make it difficult for donors to obtain accurate feedback from those they support. As philanthropist Jeff Raikes shares: "When I became the CEO of the Bill & Melinda Gates Foundation and was responsible for a multi-billion-dollar annual payout, I suddenly learned how smart, funny, and handsome I was. We realized how hard it is to get critical feedback from non-profit leaders, so a question we started asking them was what is the one thing our founda- tion could do, or do differently, that would help make your work better? This kind of question helped to even the playing field and led to conversations where we were able to learn more from our nonprofit partners."

Donors must be both self-aware and humble to ask questions like these and build trusting relationships with grantees. Flattery from nonprofits can distort a funder's view, especially when there is little market pressure to perform well with philanthropy. Perhaps because positive news can flow more freely than disappointing news, most donors report that they are highly satisfied with their current giving and not inclined to make changes.[20]

ADDITIONAL CHALLENGES FOR THE WEALTHY

Those with wealth face additional barriers to giving. Many feel like they are being watched closely, and are concerned with reputational risk associated with the gifts they make. Larger donations make headlines, and can set off a wave of both praise and criticism. As an extreme example, when Jeff and MacKenzie Bezos recently announced their plans to give $2 billion to charity, Twitter lit up with comments such as these:

- About 2% of their wealth. Nice but not a sacrifice. Many Americans give that much or more.

- Charity begins at home. Pay your warehouse workers more, have better working conditions. Or do you prefer to squeeze them in order to have more to give away?

- A 2-billion-dollar tax write-off is nothing compared to the taxes you did not pay. Public relations stunt.

Few nonprofit organizations are ready to accept extremely large donations. I encountered one individual who was planning to make a $1 billion legacy gift to his university until he learned that the 5-year fundraising goal for the entire school was only twice that amount. He stepped back his gift, realizing that his alma mater wasn't ready for a donation of the scale he had been contemplating.

If one has substantial wealth, it can be difficult to give away money fast enough. A headline from the Chronicle of Philanthropy reads "2017 Was a Banner Year, With 3 Gifts of $1 Billion or More."[21] The combined wealth of these three families was $165 billion in 2017.[22] With the markets up over 25% that year, these families stood to earn over $40 billion from their investments. Taking into account dividends and interest, it is likely that it only took about two months to earn back the $7.5 billion donated with these three banner gifts.

It is not necessary to be a billionaire to experience some of these barriers. It's normal to care about one's appearance in the community or to be concerned with "getting it right" with one's charitable investments. And the same market forces are in effect for millionaires as for uber-wealthy individuals.

Consider the following example of a person with $10 million who wishes to donate half of her wealth during her lifetime, and leave half of her money to her children. In this example, assume she gives away 10% of her wealth each year, and gets an average market return on her investments of 7% annually.

At first, it may seem like this individual would give away $5 million (half her wealth), but in reality she will need to give away $14.2 million over 20 years to achieve her charitable goal. And this example doesn't take into account any potential additional income whatsoever, beyond some market returns on her current savings.

YEAR	STARTING AMOUNT	CHARITABLE GIVING	AMOUNT AFTER GIFT	7% MARKET RETURN	YEAR-END AMOUNT
1	$10M	$1M	$9M	$630K	$9.6M
2	$9.6M	$960K	$8.7M	$607K	$9.3M
3	$9.3M	$937K	$8.3M	$584K	$8.9M
18	$5.3M	$527K	$4.7M	$332K	$5.1M
19	$4.9M	$507K	$4.6M	$320K	$4.9M

III. THE EPICENTER GIVING SYSTEM™

Based on decades of experience in the nonprofit sector, I have developed a system to overcome barriers to giving and achieve world-changing results with philanthropy. The Epicenter Giving System™ has four phases, represented by the acronym EPIC:

1) **Establish** your focus area

2) **Plan** to give

3) **Invest** in nonprofits

4) **Course-Correct** your efforts

The Epicenter Giving System™ is designed as a "cycle" in which these four phases are repeated over time. Establish. Plan. Invest. Course-correct. It takes time and energy to go through each stage of the cycle, but using the system will help anyone become a **Seismic Philanthropist** and create earth-shattering impact with their giving.

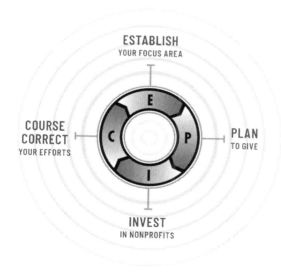

PHASE 1. ESTABLISH YOUR FOCUS AREA

The first phase of the Epicenter Giving System™ is to establish your focus, your passion, your legacy.

Many donors practice "peanut butter" philanthropy—spreading their gifts thinly across dozens of issues. By distributing their donations in this way, they never have a deep impact anywhere. Peanut butter donors feel good because they rarely have to say "no" to requests, but the lack of focus can also lead to ineffectiveness and apathy for such donors. Sadly, one study found significant disparity between issues that concern donors and the issues that they are actually supporting.[23]

To establish your focus, start by making a list of every cause you care about. Make a long and all-inclusive list. Think of life experiences that have influenced you deeply—times of great joy or great sorrow. If your child had an emergency and an EMT swept in to help, then add your local fire department to the list. If you were moved by squalid conditions when vacationing in an underdeveloped country, then add a global development organization to your list.

Next, cross off every charity for which you are unwilling to ask for friends' support, spend time volunteering, or call in political favors. You have many additional ways to help a cause than just making donations, and if you really want to have seismic impact, you'll eventually want to leverage the full weight of your time, talents, ideas, and networks. When you are done crossing off organizations, you'll have a much shorter list that offers insights into what could become your primary giving focus.

Do this exercise with your partner if you have one, and possibly with other family members as well. Discovering where your passions overlap can lead to enriching conversations with those you love, and is a great way to engage them in your philanthropic journey.

As you start to narrow down your focus, read about your issue voraciously and visit related nonprofits to gain insights from leaders in the field. What do they think are the most seismic changes that need to happen, and what is necessary to trigger such transformational shockwaves? Don't presume you have the answers before gaining input from others. Serve as a volunteer and you'll learn a great deal about an organization's work from behind the scenes.

Once you've arrived at your primary focus area, go even deeper. If you have chosen to address homelessness, try to avoid broad statements such as "I want to end homelessness." Such an expansive goal makes it challenging for even the wealthiest of donors to succeed. Instead, drill down on the issue by asking yourself questions such as these:

◉ Where do you want to tackle homelessness (perhaps a specific city or region)?

◉ Is there a particular subset of homeless

32

people you wish to serve (e.g. children, veterans, women)?

- What is working effectively in other regions to address this problem?

- Do you want to focus on immediate needs (e.g. shelter and meals) or root causes (e.g. poverty, employment and substance abuse)?

- What is your "theory of change" (nonprofit speak for the logic model you believe will bring about change)? What do you think will truly solve the problem? More beds and shelters? Mental health services? Substance abuse counseling? Low-cost housing?

The fundamental point is that **Seismic Philanthropy** is not like picking stocks. To achieve remarkable impact, don't try to create a balanced portfolio with diversified giving areas. Instead, pick an issue that means a great deal to you and then go deep. You can always preserve a small portion of your budget to support disasters as they arise, or to give socially when asked by a friend or family member. But plan to give most of your philanthropic budget to the issue you care about most.

2. PLAN TO GIVE

The second phase of the Epicenter Giving System™ is to plan your giving, define success and get laser-focused on how to get there.

Once you've locked in your issue, it's time to plan. **Seismic Philanthropy** requires strategic thinking. Two of the biggest questions you'll want to answer are how you will make gifts and who will help you make them.

FIRST: HOW?

The following is a short list of questions to think about as you establish your giving strategy. There are many more to consider, but this is a good place to start:

- How often throughout the year will you make gifts?

- How complex will your application process be for grantees?

- Will you make multi-year commitments to organizations?

- How will you interact with grantees? Will you meet with them personally or only correspond with them from a distance?

- Will you give anonymously (perhaps through a donor advised fund) or will you lend your name to the causes you support?

- What reporting and evaluation will you require of grantees?

- Will you only fund nonprofit organizations, or will you also support individuals and for-profit companies that advance your goals?

There are pros and cons to each of these questions and the way you answer them has considerable implications. Unless you have experience working in the nonprofit arena, consider hiring an expert to provide context and help you understand the impact of your choices. If you lack enthusiasm for the operational side of making grants, there are many resources available to help you. These include software that has been developed to process grants, consulting firms that serve as the back-office for foundations, donor-advised funds, and private consultants. In addition, multi-family offices that help support families on a variety of needs frequently help their clients with philanthropy.

Regardless of your strategy, make sure you always kick the tires when making donations. You wouldn't buy a car without taking a test ride first, yet the majority of philanthropists act before appropriately researching organizations. Although most donors say they want to be strategic with their giving, only a third conduct any research at all, and a scant 6% compare nonprofits before making a donation.[24]

NEXT: WHO?

It is important to decide who will join you in making grant decisions. Involving family members can be a way to build intergenerational relationships. However, many with great wealth don't want their children to know the extent of their fortune. Others find that they have different political and social values from family members. If this is your case, consider finding a skilled consultant who can help your family find common ground on your giving priorities.

Because philanthropy is so deeply connected to one's personal values, new donors often turn first to someone they implicitly trust for support—a relative, close friend, or business colleague. This can be a flawed strategy if you seek to have seismic impact. If you had to have a complex medical surgery, would you choose

your aunt, best friend, or coworker to perform the operation? Probably not, unless that
person also happens to be a surgeon. You may
want help in preparing for foundation board
meetings, facilitating family retreats, conduct-
ing due diligence of nonprofits, and other as-
pects of grant making. If so, hire a professional
guide who has been down this path before.

You will find other valuable partners by
looking closely at those doing work on the
ground. Seek to build mindful, respectful
relationships with grantees so you can truly
learn from each other. Tackle the power dy-
namic head-on, and approach grantees as experts and peers.

Consider collaborating with other funders as
well. There is a proverb inscribed on a wall at
the Bill & Melinda Gates Foundation: "If you
want to go fast, go alone. If you want to go
far, go together." If the largest foundation in
the world believes it can't solve substantive
issues alone, the same is almost certainly true

38

for you. For any serious challenge, you can be sure that others have already spent significant money and energy trying to tackle the issue. If you want to turbocharge your learning and planning, talk with other donors to learn from their experiences. The social sector is far more collaborative than the corporate arena, and others will typically be willing to share their successes and roadblocks. Be reasonable about what your resources can accomplish, and if you want to take on big meaty issues, partner with others to get the job done.

3. INVEST IN NONPROFITS

The third phase of the Epicenter Giving System™ is the most fun—making investments in nonprofits.

Making actual investments seems like it should be the easiest part of the cycle (you simply write some checks), but it is also where many donors get stuck. Research shows that people become more stressed when facing uncertain outcomes than when they know bad things will definitely occur.[25] Naturally, we shy away from committing ourselves to the unknown even after all our careful planning.

In phase three of the cycle, it is time to either cook or get out of the philanthropic kitchen. At the moment you make a donation, you will never be 100% sure that your investment will accomplish its goals. Even though you can't guarantee success with every donation, you can take heart in knowing that you have done your homework. You will have established your focus area and planned thoroughly. Moreover, you'll still have a chance to course-correct in the future as you learn from the experience of giving.

4. COURSE-CORRECT YOUR EFFORTS

The fourth phase of the Epicenter Giving System[TM] is to course-correct your strategy before starting the cycle again.

Passions can change over time, and your giving priorities may change too. You won't often shift your focus area, but you might refine your approach based on what you learn. Perhaps you'll move away from tackling an issue's root cause toward addressing its most pressing current needs. Or maybe you'll change your geographic focus from one region to another.

On rare occasions, you might develop an entirely new focus area because life experiences can change perspective. For example, many people become passionate about funding medical research when a loved one is diagnosed with a disease.

Some donors establish rules that limit how many years in a row they will support a nonprofit organization, often because they don't want nonprofits to become dependent on them for funding. Although you have the right to do as you wish, this may not be the best strategy. You don't stop eating at a restaurant you like, in order to keep its owners from becoming too dependent on you as a customer. With philanthropy, you have important goals that you wish to accomplish. If a nonprofit organization is adeptly helping you meet your goals, consider funding it repeatedly year after year. You might even reserve a portion of your budget to help grantees when they face unanticipated needs with their work.

Very few if any one-time gifts have seismic effect. Providing multi-year ongoing support at meaningful levels is usually required to accomplish big goals. Take the long view when engaging with nonprofit organizations, and think holistically about how your gifts will best create change. If you are investing in buildings, think about funding the programs that will take place in those structures. If your giving helps develop a cure for a disease, consider funding the commercialization and dissemination of that cure. If you are donating art to a museum, consider paying for the cost of storing, maintaining and curating the art in the future.

If you acknowledge from the beginning that you will be supporting an issue over the long haul, it is easier to accept that you are going to make some mistakes along the way with your philanthropic gifts. Assume that your giving will never be perfect, and aim to constantly improve your approach.

You will need to be your own worst critic at times, holding yourself accountable for the quality of your giving. To do so, ask yourself questions such as these:

- What is working with your philanthropic investments and what is not achieving your goals? Why?

- What have you learned from the grants you've made and your interactions in the field?

- Are you asking your grantees to measure the results that matter most?

- Are you interacting with grantees in the way you would like?

If exploring these questions seems daunting, there are evaluation experts who can help—ranging from independent advisors to staff of community foundations to national consulting firms.

ENTER THE CYCLE AGAIN

After assessing your own effectiveness, it's time to cycle through the Epicenter Giving System™ again. Revisit your focus and strategy, and then make more grants. Over time, the process will become easier, because you'll gain clarity about which of your investments are driving the change you want to see.

Seismic Philanthropy is not for the faint of heart. It requires a willingness to be introspective and vulnerable while establishing your focus area; courage to say "no" to many who ask for support; curiosity to learn from others along the way; patience to involve family members in your journey; and humility to recognize and learn from your mistakes as well as your wins. But the change you envision is well worth it. Commit yourself to becoming a **Seismic Philanthropist,** and seize the opportunity today to ignite positive change for you, your loved ones, and the greater world.

REFERENCES

1   99WMFK "Michigan Hero: Edward N Hines 1870-1938"

2   Mining Foundation Southwest

3   http://mailtribune.com/business/fog-lines-invented-in-early-50s

4   https://cspcs.sanford.duke.edu/

5   https://data.bls.gov/cgi-bin/cpicalc.pl

6   "The Gospel of Wealth" by Andrew Carnegie, 1889

7   World Health Organization Fact Sheet; The Top 10 Causes of Death

8   WWF

9   UNHCR, UN Refugee Agency

10 Greenpeace

11 National Alliance to End Homelessness

12 DoSomething.org

13 Dunn et. al, 2009

14 Moll et. al, 2006

15 Iyengar and Lepper, 2000

16 US Trust Study of the Philanthropy Conversation, 2018

17 Good to Great and the Social Sector, 2005

18 Stanford GSR Excellence Website, Nov 8, 2017

19 Forbes, "Five Dangerous Lessons to Learn from Steve Jobs," 2011

20 Camber Collective "Money For Good" Report, 2015

21 Chronicle of Philanthropy, Jan 2, 2018

22 Forbes Richest People List and Richest in Tech List, 2017

23 Chicago Community Trust "On the Table" Report, 2016

24 Hope Consulting "Money For Good" Report, 2011

25 Greco and Rogers, 2003

54400938R00033

Made in the USA
Middletown, DE
13 July 2019